Good Morning Gorgeous

Good Morning Gorgeous

❧

A GUIDE TO HAVING AN INTIMATE RELATIONSHIP WITH YOUR HEAVENLY FATHER

Angel Casillas

Casillas Coaching

For the young lady who longs to have a close relationship with
their father,
I pray that God ministers to you while you read,
just as He ministered to me while I wrote.

"My purpose in writing is to encourage you & assure that what
you are experiencing is truly part of God's grace for you.
Stand firm in this grace." 1 Peter 5:12

Contents

1

~

Good Morning Gorgeous

It's morning, and your phone is vibrating. It's a text from someone special saying, "Good morning, gorgeous." The muscles in your face wake up, and you manage to smile brightly, simply because of three words. On any given day, a "Good morning" text could be just what you need to jumpstart your day, especially when it's from that special someone. That text could be the thing that brings you joy and motivates you to have a great day.

Imagine this book as your "Good morning" text from God. God wants to do the same thing to your life that a good morning text does for your morning, but the effects of God's "Good morning gorgeous" will fill your entire life with joy. Consider this a love letter from God to one of His favorite girls explaining who He is and how to be in a relationship with Him. As you read this book, I pray that you start to learn yourself, who you are, and whose you are. You may not feel perfect or important, but according to God's plan for your life, you are the perfect vessel to fulfill the important purpose that He has created just for you. To God, there's no one else in the world more important than you because He designed you for a specific thing, and He wants to make sure that you accomplish it. If you have not yet found what that purpose is, I pray that God will reveal it to you.

God designed humans to be relational, meaning that relationships are essential for survival. Most things we do, and who we are as individuals, relate to the relationships we had or have in our lives. Throughout this book, I will connect your relationship with God with the other relationships you're in so you can better understand how to have a working relationship with God. Many times, looking at something from a natural perspective makes it easier for you to understand the spiritual perspective.

When you think of your relationship with God, what comes to mind? How do you view God? Who is He to you? Now is not the time to think about all the super deep things you heard in church about God. Instead, I am asking you to take some time to think about who God is to you as an individual. Think about the situations that God brought you through; how did He make you feel during that time? When you were lonely, was God a friend? When you need to be comforted, can you see Him as a comforting father? When you aren't feeling loved, can He be the love of your life? It's ok if you can't put who God has been to you into words yet, but by the end of reading this book, I pray that God reveals who He has been to you and who He wants to be for you.

For me, God is all of the previously mentioned things. He is my friend, He's my comforter, my protector, and the love of my life, but most importantly, He is my father. None of those relational aspects came easy. I didn't wake up one day and know everything about being in a relationship with a supreme invisible being. I had to teach myself how to find God and be in a relationship with Him. The moment that I learned how to have a personal relationship with God was when my life changed. You read that right; I had to learn how to have a personal relationship with God. And just being honest, I am still learning as I'm typing.

Just like natural relationships take time and effort, your spiritual relationship with God requires time and effort. Connections don't just magically happen. No one has ever met anyone and instantly had the perfect relationship, no matter what anyone tries to tell you. I've known my husband longer than I haven't known him, and we are still learning each other. Jesus was perfect. He was the son of God, and He didn't even "just click" with anyone. His disciples ate and slept with Him for years, and they still didn't know everything about Him. But what they did know about Him, they learned over time. In the same way, it takes you a while to learn your partner in any relationship; it takes time to learn our Heavenly Father.

I'm a spades player, and anyone who plays spades knows that it's better to play with someone you've played with for a while than someone you just met. Spades is a game of strategy, so it's best to pick a partner and stay with them because the right partner will learn how you play and will make moves based on how you move. In my life, I've had two consistent spades partners, my cousin and my girl from high school. Every time we sit down to play, I watch how they hold their cards, their body language, and the tone of their voice. All of these things help me strategize. Based on those things alone, I can tell if my partner has a good hand or not. Eventually, we got to a point where we became so in sync we could predict what suit we wanted each other to play next. Because of how observant we are of each other, beating us is rare. Learning my partner made it easier for us to win. Good Morning Gorgeous (GMG) exists to help you understand the most incredible partner you'll ever have so you can win at life!

It takes time to understand your partner so be patient and do not rush yourself, or rush through this book. You'll get the most from GMG if you take your time. At the end of each chapter, I included a few journaling questions. The questions are for your benefit, so be honest with yourself. Take time to think about what you read and study the scriptures provided in each chapter. Self-reflection is one of the best resources for growth.

After reading each chapter, grab a journal and a pen, take time to reflect on what you read, and spend some quality quiet time with God. I've also included prayers at the end of every chapter to seal what you learned in your heart and jumpstart your next conversation with your Heavenly Father. Hopefully, you'll learn more about yourself and develop a better understanding of who God has been to you and who He wants to be to you as we go on this journey together. Keep in mind that life is about progress not perfection. The things you learn from this book will take time to become habits, so don't feel discouraged when you think you're not living up to expectation, God's not through with you yet!

Chapter 1 Journaling Questions

What is one thing you are looking forward to learning from reading this book?

What do you think will be the most challenging part of developing an intimate relationship with God?

"Dear Heavenly Father, you're such a great and powerful God. I thank you for allowing me to come to you as your daughter through your Son, Jesus Christ. I am taking a leap of faith, and I am asking you to meet me here. Please help me understand and retain the information that I read. Please be with me as I go on this self-awareness and spiritual development journey. I know that as long as I walk with You, You will protect me and keep me from harm. I love you, Daddy, thank you for everything, Amen".

2

~

Relationship

Many Christians claim to be saved, sanctified, and filled with the Holy Ghost but have no idea what it means to have a personal relationship with God. I have been going to church my entire life, and I learned how to sound saved quicker than I learned how to live saved. It took me a while to live the lifestyle God required of me because I didn't know how to integrate my relationship with God with my everyday life.

The saints are loud and bold when they tell you the importance of having a personal relationship with your Lord and Savior, Jesus Christ. Unfortunately, many ministries have not been able to teach the younger generations how to be in a relationship with the most magnificent being in the Universe. In no way am I trying to bad-mouth any ministry. Instead of merely pointing out a problem, I wrote GMG, hoping to be a part of the change. I believe that people will benefit greater from teaching that is applicable, practical, and direct. Our job is not only to point people to Christ, but we also have to show them how to be with Christ in a world that does not put Him first.

I'm a church baby, meaning I've been in church since I came out of my mother's womb. I gave my life to Christ when I was seven. It was the year nineteen hundred and ninety-five, and I remember it like it was yesterday. My ears were burning, tears flowed down my face, and there were millions of butterflies in my stomach. The children's ministry head at the time prayed for me. As he prayed, I could feel a sense of comfort and peace wrapping around me. It felt like a weighted blanket. It made me feel safe and comfortable, like climbing in bed with your granny under the forty blankets she has. After he prayed, I stood up in front of the congregation, proud as ever.

I honestly wish that moment would've lasted forever, but unfortunately, life happens. As you grow, life becomes more challenging. The teenage years smack you in the face and turn you into someone no one recognizes, not even yourself. I never left the church, but I put my salvation in my back pocket, only to take it out on church days. People knew I was saved, but my relationship with God wasn't my priority. I loved God, but I did not understand what it truly meant to have a relationship with Him. At that time, going to church to see my friends was way more important than trying to figure out an invisible being. (No disrespect intended). Now that I understand how to get the most out of my relationship with my Heavenly Father, I wish I had made an effort to establish one earlier in my life. It would have saved me from so much trouble.

He Wants A Connection With You

The dictionary defines the word relationship in three ways, and I believe that all three ways relate to the types of relationships we can have with God. The first definition of the word relationship is a connection, association, or involvement[1] God desires to have a connection with you. He wants to be associated with you, meaning, when people see you, He wants them to see Him. I know you've heard someone say, "When you see him, know that's me!" You can find a rendition of the quote in John 12:45 (NKJV), Jesus says, "Whoever sees me, sees the one who sent me." Jesus was on Earth when He said that, and we know that His Father, God sent Him. So when you see Jesus, you're seeing our Heavenly Father, God.

God wants to be so connected with you that when people see you, they notice that there's something different about you. They should see that there's something that makes you stand out from the rest. There's a movie where the main character finds the power within and literally glows. When you connect to God, His power doesn't give you a literal glow, but God's Spirit gives you a spiritual glow that makes you more attractive and more noticeable. When you allow God's power to live inside of you, you glow from within, and that's what makes you stand out.

The key to your relationship with God is giving God an invitation to join you. God doesn't need to force himself on you to make Himself feel good. He's a King! Can you imagine being King of everything and having to beg or force your way into your subjects' homes? That's not Kingly behavior. That's what Tyrants do, and God is far from being a Tyrant; he's full of love. He desires to love you dearly and to protect and provide for you. He would rather wait for you to come to Him. He might allow some things to cross your path that will speed up the process of you coming to Him, but He will never force himself on you. You must choose to serve God (we'll get into choosing God in more detail later on).

As a teenager, I put God on the shelf and kept Him separate from my everyday life. I still loved Him, but I didn't love Him the way He desired me to love Him. God wanted to be a part of every part of my life, and I took that away from Him by only allowing Him to have me when He was convenient for me. I didn't realize that what I put up on the shelf was my most significant advantage; it was everything that I needed and more.

Imagine you're at a crowded amusement park, you're three feet tall, and everyone around you is over five feet. You can't see anything but a bunch of butts, but then your dad, who's six-five, picks you up and puts you on his shoulders. Now you can see over all the people, and you might even be able to see the other side of the park. When you were on the ground, you couldn't see what was around you because you weren't tall enough, so you had no idea what you were missing until you took advantage of your dad's shoulders. In this scenario, your dad placing you on his shoulders gives you an edge over the people around you. You can now see what you couldn't see before. When you give God an invitation to join you every day, it's like He's placing you on His shoulders. Being involved with God is the advantage you never knew you needed until you actually use the advantage.

Connected by Blood & by Marriage

The second definition of relationship is a connection between persons by blood or marriage. Not sure if you know this, but we are connected to God by blood and marriage. It sounds strange, but it's true. The Bible refers to Jesus as the *Bridegroom* (John 3:29), and the church is *His Bride* (Ephesians 5:22-33). The church in this context does not mean the literal building we attend, but it's referring to the people that love God. We love God, so we are the church; therefore, we are Jesus' bride, making us connected to God by marriage.

The Bible uses marriage as an example of the relationship that God wants to have with you. You can look at practically any scripture that deals with marriage and replace wife with the church because that's a comparison that God established in Ephesians 5:22-33. Here's an excerpt from the Message bible, but make sure you check out the rest of the passage:

"Husbands, go all out in your love for your wives, exactly as Christ did for the church—a love marked by giving, not getting. Christ's love makes the church whole. His words evoke her beauty. Every- thing he does and says is designed to bring the best out of her, dressing her in dazzling white silk, radiant with holiness. And that is how husbands ought to love their wives. They're really doing themselves a favor—since they're already 'one' in marriage."

For this particular scripture, I enjoy how the Message Bible beauti- fully illustrated how Christ loves the church. I love how it explains how Christ loves the church in comparison to the way husbands should love their wives; it makes His love more practical. "Christ's love makes the church whole" is an excellent way of showing that with- out Christ, we are missing something, and once we have Him, we are whole. I tell people all the time that I'm just Angel on my own, and that's cool, but now that I am with my husband (that I waited on God for), I feel more whole. I feel as though now that we have become one, I've become more confident in who I am. I'm more secure as an indi- vidual because I feel like I have someone who accepts me and has my back no matter what. Another part of the passage can support how I feel: "Everything He does and says is designed to bring the best out of her." The same way a husband is supposed to help his wife be the best she can, God has given us instruction that is purposed to make us live our best lives. God will never provide you with instruction that will cause you harm. That's not His nature. Isaiah 63:9 (NLT) shows us the type of God we serve:

"In all their suffering He also suffered, and He personally

rescued them. In His love and mercy, He redeemed them. He lifted them up and carried them through all the years."

Does that sound like the type of God that would intentionally bring you harm? It seems to me like He would much rather put Himself in harm's way before He allows anything to hurt us. Notice that the scripture said that He suffers when we suffer. Someone who hurts when we hurt would not intentionally cause us pain because that would mean He would be causing Himself pain.

We are also connected to God by His blood because of the blood of the Lamb, Jesus Christ. God's Son shed His blood on the cross for us. So Ephesians tells us that we are close to God only because of the blood of His Son Jesus (Ephesians 2:13). Many other scriptures let us know that the blood of the Lamb purchased us, but Acts 20:28 (ESV) is very clear about the situation.

"Pay careful attention to yourselves and to all the flock, in which the Holy Spirit has made you overseers, to care for the church of God, which He obtained by His own blood."

Connected Because of Love

The third definition explains a relationship as an emotional or other connection between people. Lastly, we have a relationship with God simply because He loves us. God loves us more than anyone could ever love someone. Romans 5:8 (ESV) tells us that "God shows His love for us in that while we were still sinners, Christ died for us." The only reason Jesus gave up His life was because his dad told Him to do it. Can you imagine telling your Son that He has to die so that other people can live? I can't even imagine putting my dog to sleep if it was a matter of life or death for someone! The love connection with

God is the most significant part of our relationship. The love that He has for us makes it possible for us to be in a relationship with Him. 1 John 4:16 (ESV) says,

"So we have come to know and to believe the love that God has for us. God is love, and whoever abides in love, abides in God, and God abides in him."

God made love require action when He established it as something you must give. As a result of the love He has for us, He had to do something to let us know how much He loves us. Let's revisit Ephesians 5:25-28 (MSG), which mentions God's love is about giving and not receiving. If you are familiar with The Five Love Languages, you could say that God's primary love language is giving. The author of The Five Love Languages, Gary Chapman, said that gifts are visual symbols of love. From the beginning, God gave us things to visually show us the love He has for us. God gave humans dominion over all of creation (Genesis 1:26). He gave Adam a wife (Genesis 2:20-25), and then He gave them children even after they disobeyed Him (Genesis 4:1-2). The most significant gift we received was a personal sacrifice. God gave us the most precious thing He had.

He gave us Jesus Christ, and then He gave us His blood. John 3:16 (NLT) states,

"For this is how God loved the world: He gave His one and only Son, so that everyone who believes in Him will not perish but have eternal life."

God is love (1 John 4:8), so when God sent Jesus as a representation of the love God has for us, He was sending a part of Himself down here to us. Your Father God sacrificed Himself, and His Son for you so you can spend eternity with Him! How amazing is that?

Chapter 2 Journaling Questions

What is/was the most significant relationship in your life?

How do you feel about the sacrifice of love that God has shown for you?

"Dear Heavenly Father, you are holy and righteous. There is no one like you. I am coming to you as your daughter, and I am asking you to meet me here. Help me understand how great your sacrifice of love was and give me a heart to want to have a deeper relationship with you. I want my relationship with You to be the most significant relationship that I have. Father, I ask that You show me how to be the daughter you desire me to be and remove anything from my life that is blocking me from having a true father-daughter relationship with You. I love you, Father, and I thank You for everything, Amen."

3

❧

Our Father

One morning, as I sat in the prayer corner of my closet praying for someone who crossed my mind, God began to speak to me concerning me. We talked about many things, but His main focus was this book and why I needed to return to writing. He didn't ask, and it wasn't a suggestion. I could tell that it was a command because of how I felt in the moment. I felt a sense of urgency. I felt God saying, "I need you to start by explaining that I am Daddy God. I need for my girls to relate to that part of me first." He didn't even give me the chance to ask why. He continued by saying, "You've seen how daddy issues change a person's perspective on life and how people respond to various situations because of their relationship with their father. Explain who I am." So with the help of His Spirit and His written word, I will try my best to show you who your Heavenly Father is.

First, let me clear one thing up. God did not talk to me like we would talk to each other. It was more like a feeling. The best way that I can explain it is when I am quiet enough, my inner dialogue becomes aligned with God's Spirit. Instead of hearing my thoughts, it's like I'm having a conversation in my mind with someone else. It's kind of like having someone else's thoughts inside my head. I don't hear them in someone else's voice, but I know they're different from my thoughts. I'll get more into it in a later chapter.

Before getting into God being your Heavenly Father, I have to clear something up first. When you think of God as Father, Daddy God, or Abba Father, you can not put your Heavenly Father in the same box as your earthly father. They are not the same. Unfortunately, many women have not had positive experiences with their earthly fathers, causing them difficulties in many areas. You may have trust issues, you might fall for the wrong type of men, or you might shut yourself off entirely from connecting with anyone.

Unresolved issues with your earthly father could distort the way you view your Heavenly Father, but we must remember that God does not follow their example no matter how we may view our earthly fathers. God is the example of a father that many fathers failed to model themselves after. When you think of God as a father, do not automatically assume that He will be like your earthly father because that's not who He's modeled after. God is the creator. He follows no one's template. I know it can be easy to put human characteristics and limitations on God, but doing that is what stops you from seeing God the way He wants you to see Him.

Many women have deep wounds because their fathers failed to love, cherish, protect, and affirm them the way that God intended. You have to realize that it is not your fault that you have daddy issues. It is not your responsibility to be a perfect daughter so your father would love you. One reason why God created you is to love and be loved by your father. That includes both of your fathers, the spiritual and the earthly ones. Your father's responsibility is to be your covering, protector, encourager, and provider. Ephesians 6:4 explains that fathers are not to provoke their children but to train and instruct them in the ways of God. It is your earthly father's responsibility to teach you right from wrong and to show you a Godly example of what love is. Your responsibility as your father's daughter is to love him with all your heart and obey him. And because of the obedience and the love you have for him, respecting him should be easy.

When it comes to the relationship you have with your earthly father, please realize that it is not your fault that you were not given the proper love and direction from your father that God intended for you to have. That was your father's choice, and because of the free will that God gives to us, it's not God's fault either (Deuteronomy 30:19-20). Unlike God, your earthly father is not perfect. A close friend asked me, "If he knows wrong, doesn't that mean he knows right?"

The simple answer is no. Parents typically model themselves after their parents. The exception comes when the child realizes that what they experienced was wrong, and they make a conscious effort to change the pattern. Unfortunately, many people repeat what they were taught and don't make an effort to improve the dysfunctional pattern. The reality of poor father-daughter relationships is that your father probably wasn't shown how to be the father you needed, so you have to give him grace. This doesn't mean you should allow him to mistreat you. It just means you should try to have compassion and understanding.

It doesn't feel right to be the bigger person in a relationship with someone older than you, but sometimes we must do it. Fortunately, we can find freedom from our broken hearts and our hurtful past in God. First, admit that you're hurt and ask God to heal your heart from whatever circumstance broke it. Next, ask your Heavenly Father to forgive you for any anger or bitterness that you may have toward your earthly father. Lastly, ask God to help you forgive him so that you can be free to love God as your father. Don't get discouraged if healing doesn't happen instantly. Healing is a process, and you have to rely on God to take you through that process, so don't feel bad if you have to ask God to help you forgive every single day.

If you have made an effort to have a relationship or repair a broken relationship, and your father was not receptive, or he didn't change, embrace your freedom and move on with your life. If the relationship caused you too much pain to have a conversation with your father, write him a letter explaining everything you wanted from him that you didn't receive and the things that hurt you. You can either send the letter to him or read it to an empty chair. Vocalizing that pain is so freeing. I've done this exercise myself, and I felt tons of weight leave my shoulders. The relationship between my father and me is non-existent at the moment, but it's not holding me back anymore. I've forgiven him, and now I am free to love and be loved by my Daddy God.

The role of a parent is to love their child unconditionally and teach and care for their child until they can take care of themself. As their child, all you have to do is love, honor, and obey your parents. Even if you did something wrong, your parents are supposed to show you what's right and love you regardless of what you do. That's the meaning of unconditional love. Your Heavenly Father wants you to know that you are His child, and there's Nothing that you can do that will get God to stop loving you or abandon you (Ephesians 1:4-8). In Deuteronomy 31:6, God promises never to leave you or forget about you. As women, our connections are vital. A part of our purpose is to compliment the man (Genesis 2:18). God designed us to need connection. So when a relationship loses its connection, it hurts us deeply. This is why many women are so broken when they don't have a nurturing relationship with their earthly father.

In Hebrews 13:5, God promises never to leave you or forget about you, but it is possible to feel like He's not there because of how you're treating Him. If God seems distant, like He's nowhere to be found, consider the amount of effort you've been putting into your relationship with Him. Are you making Him a priority, or is your relationship with Him based on convenience?

Abba Father

When people pray, they say, "Father God," but what does that even mean? The first thing that may come to someone's mind is God's role in the Holy Trinity. God is Jesus' father, but we should be able to go a little further than that. In the Bible, Jesus refers to God as Abba Father in Mark 14:36. Abba is Aramaic for Father. It is one of the most intimate names given to God. Jesus and Paul are the only ones in the Bible who used the term, and they both had extremely close and familiar relationships with God.

Paul said that because we have been adopted as God's children and not his slaves, we get to call God Abba (Romans 8:15). If anyone believes that Jesus died on the cross to save their soul, then they have the right to call God Abba Father. Once you believe that Jesus is the son of God, you have been reborn into His family, and because of your new birthright, you are now a child of the Most High. Since you're a daughter of the Most High, you are royalty. Being God's daughter gives you access to parts of God and His Kingdom that aren't available to everyone.

I've heard people say that's my father, not my Daddy, when referring to their earthly father because of the type of relationship they have with him. When you say father, you're acknowledging the fact that he is your parent. When you say Daddy, you're expressing an intimate relationship with your father. A Daddy is someone a daughter loves dearly, someone you admire, and someone you think is the biggest, strongest, and bravest man in the world. To put it plain and simple, the term Daddy suggests a close relationship.

When I need to talk to the Daddy part of God, I call him Daddy or say Daddy God. There are times when I need to feel his presence as my Daddy, and I want to make sure that He knows who I need Him to be at that moment. When I need fatherly guidance, comfort, provision, or protection, I imagine myself climbing in my Daddy God's lap. I give him big puppy dog eyes and ask Him exactly what I want. God gave you the ability to tug on his heart (Matthew 7:7). Never forget that you have that ability. He gave it to you for a reason.

Think of it like this: God is King, and because you're God's daughter, you are now Princess (insert your name here). And because God is King, anything in the Kingdom is yours. You're not some random village person or a foreigner from another land. You are God's chosen. In earthly father-daughter relationships, little girls have been given the ability to have their Daddy wrapped around their finger. That means they can almost get away with everything and ask for anything. As long as their father has the power to make it happen, he will. The same thing is true with our Heavenly Father. As long as it's in His Kingdom, it's yours.

Luke 12:32 (NKJV) tells us, "It is your Father's good pleasure to give you the Kingdom." God wants to give you what you ask for, but what you ask for has to help God fulfill His plan on the earth. Although we have plans in our mind, God's plan is the only one that matters (Proverbs 19:21).

And that is what God uses to bless us. Unlike an earthly father who will give without considering the future effect of the gift, God has a plan for everything He does. God isn't going to give you anything that He knows will take you off the path He has for you. Our prayers often go unanswered because we ask for things without considering whether or not it is a part of God's desire for our life. Sometimes we ask for something just because we want it instead of realizing that it may be harmful or not the right time.

When I was 22 years old, I desperately sought God because I wanted to be in a relationship so bad. I had been hanging out with someone I thought was special, but things weren't quite working out. I knew I wasn't ready for marriage, but I just wanted someone I could call my own. So before bed one night, I asked God, "Can I have a boy-friend, please?" As I began to fall asleep, I could've sworn I heard my grandmother calling me, but unfortunately, she passed when I was seven, so I knew it wasn't her.

I waited to see if God was trying to get my attention because, in 1 Samuel 3:2-10, God called out to Samuel and thought his master Eli was calling him. Eventually, Eli realized that God was trying to speak to Samuel, so he told Samuel to wait and listen to what God had to say. After I realized that God might be trying to get my attention, I grabbed a pen and my journal and eagerly waited to hear from Him. I felt God say, "If I give him to you now, you'll mess each other up."

I was glad to get such a quick response to my question, so I figured I'd ask another one, "Have I met him yet?" and God answered me and said, "Yes." That was good enough for me. A few weeks later, someone I trusted blessed me with a word, and she said that I had already met my husband, and she saw me married at 28 years old.

When I asked God for a boyfriend, I had just started getting myself back on track to being the woman God called me to be, and I didn't need any distractions. God was rebranding the life that I messed up by doing my own thing for years, so I had no business asking Him for one of His children so I could mess him up too. But since He loved me, He gave me an answer that would hold me over until the set time. I was done with just dating for fun, but I wasn't ready to be someone's wife. Honestly, I wasn't even sure if I wanted to be anyone's wife, notice that I asked God for a boyfriend and not a husband.

I spent the next few years focused on growing in Christ. But, I didn't just sit in my room and wait for my husband to fall out of the sky. During that time, on top of studying scriptures that would build me up and direct me, I read a lot of inspirational books. Some of the most helpful books I read were *The Five Love Languages* by Gary Chapman, *Just Enough Light for the Step I'm On*, and *The Power of a Praying Woman* by Stormie Omartian, and *The Law of Confession, The Kingdom of God in You, Transform Your Thinking* by Bill Winston. Those books and a few others changed how my life was going. The way I talked changed, and how I viewed myself and the world around me changed. I found answers to many of my questions, and I also answered some of the questions the people around me had. After educating myself on the things of the Kingdom, I noticed that people started gravitating towards me. As someone who never really liked being bothered with people, it took some getting used to. But, eventually, I realized that you can't stop people from being drawn to the God in you, so I embraced it.

After allowing God to change me from the inside out, the guy I thought was special when I was twenty-two also noticed my growth. He had grown a lot during that time, and in 2016, two months after my twenty-eighth birthday, we got married. When I asked God for a boyfriend, He already knew who my husband was. Neither one of us were ready, so to save us from ourselves, we had to wait. I constantly tell my husband that I am so glad that we waited on God. Looking back at who we were back then, I know our marriage wouldn't be as rewarding as it is now. God knew the kind of woman my husband needed, and at twenty-two, I was not her. God also knew that the lifestyle my husband lived at the time was attractive to me, and I wouldn't have made him change because a bad boy that goes to church is way more exciting than a safe church boy. God's timing and His plan will always be better than anything we could come up with. I am so grateful that my Heavenly Father has my best interest in mind and answered my prayer in His time and not mine.

Chapter 3 Journaling Questions

What was your relationship like with your earthly father?

Do you think that the relationship you have/had with your earthly father positively or negatively affects your ability to view God as Father? Explain your answer.

Are there things that you need to forgive your father for? If so, write them down (you don't have to share them).

"Dear Heavenly Father, thank you for being a loving and patient Father. Thank you for allowing me to come to you as your daughter. I am so thankful that you're not like man, and I can trust you with my heart. Daddy God, I am coming to you today with my heart exposed and asking that you heal the parts of me that are hurting and broken. I need your help forgiving my earthly father for (insert what you're asking help to forgive). Father, I also ask that you heal me from all the things that have broken my heart. I know that you are a loving and forgiving God and because I am your daughter, I have the power to love and forgive too. I ask that you take this hurt, anger, bitterness, and sadness from me so that I can embrace your joy and your peace. Give me a loving spirit so that these things don't cause me to harden my heart. Let me learn to love you how a daughter should love her father without fear of being hurt or disappointed. I love you Daddy, thank you for everything, Amen.

4

∾

Desire, Intimacy & Vulnerability

Desire

One of my mentees asked me, "How do you know if someone is interested in you?" I told them to watch the person's behavior. Desire is a verb, which means it requires action. A person's behavior will let you know without a shadow of a doubt if someone is genuinely interested in you. Someone who truly desires you will not just say things because they sound good. They'll show you that they want you. There should be no need to question someone's interest in you because their effort usually shows you.

The most important thing that God did to prove His interest in you was send His only son down to this ghetto planet to be disrespected, beaten, and killed so you don't have to go to Hell and spend the rest of eternity smelling like sulfur. God sent His son, a literal part of Him, down to Earth to save your undeserving soul so you can live with Him for all of eternity. That is the most significant sacrifice that anyone will ever make in the name of love. If you look at how you interact with God, do your actions show him how thankful you are for His sacrifice? If God was not Alpha and Omega, would He be able to tell that you desire him solely based on your actions? For example, during praise and worship, how's your posture? Are you standing honoring God, or are you seated with your arms folded? When you pray, are you giving him your undivided attention, or are you trying to multitask? Desire is a strong feeling of wanting that is vital in any relationship.

Desire is such a vital part of our relationship with God that you can see it throughout the Bible. Psalm 63 shows how truly thirsty David was for God. David was a man created after God's heart. If there's anyone you should model yourself after, it would be him (minus the murder and adultery parts). If you have not read the full story of David (1 & 2 Samuel), I suggest you carve out some time and check that out. Once you read his story, in its entirety, then you'll be able to understand and empathize with David when you read the Psalms he wrote. David wrote some of the most powerful verses during his most difficult challenges. Saul was so envious of the anointing and the favor of God that was on David that he wanted him dead. So David had to run for his life. Can you imagine being hunted by your best friend's father for four years only because God liked you?

Anyway, when David wrote Psalm 63, he was hiding from Saul, and it was a challenging time for David. So instead of moaning and groaning and complaining to people he met, David called out to God. When David said, "early will I seek thee; my soul thirsts for thee, my flesh longs for thee," I don't think David was only speaking of a specific time of day. I believe that he was saying that he would talk to God first. In this chapter, David explains his desire for God. David wanted God to know how important He was to Him. By saying he'll seek him early, David wanted to clarify that there was no one else that he would put before God. That's the type of relationship we should have with our Heavenly Father. A relationship where God knows that we put Him first and that we want Him more than anything else in the world.

David's choice of words was so descriptive; they were perfect! He said, "my soul thirst for thee, my flesh longs for thee." I can imagine David, in hiding, on his knees, physically crying out to the Lord, in desperate need of God's provision. Picture yourself alone, in a desert on the hottest day in history. You haven't had any food or water in four days. You're weak, your mouth is dry, your lips are crusty, and your skin is rough and ashy. How desperate would you be for water? That's how thirsty David was for God. David believed that if God did not help him through his situation, he would die.

When it comes to our relationship with God, we have to have the same urgent desire for God as David had, or as we would have for water in the previous desert scenario. We have to know that we won't make it if God does not help us through our situations. A desperate desire for our Heavenly Father has to become a lifestyle and not just when you need Him to work something out for you. If you increase your desire for your Heavenly Father, a more rewarding relationship is waiting for you with Him.

Intimacy

Jeremiah 24:7 says, "I will give them a heart to know me." In this sentence, the word, know, is not the, Hey, I know her that we're used to. This know means to be intimate with. Being intimate does not mean let's have sex. Sex is not intimacy, although it can be a result of intimacy. Intimacy refers to having a personal, familiar, and cozy closeness with someone. I heard a teaching that explained intimacy and broke the word down to: into me see. When you say you're in an intimate relationship, it means that you see into a person, and you allow them to see into you. Seeing into someone means that you can see the real version of who someone is. You can't say that you know someone until you have experienced their soul. Until you experience someone's soul, you only know what they have allowed you to see.

A person's soul is the most authentic part of them; it's their total self. Think of your soul as the selfie you take without the filter. When you share your soul with someone, you give them your complete self without the extra razzle-dazzle that makes you look better than you really are. To be intimate with someone, you have to allow them to see all of your scars, weaknesses, and imperfections. Whoever you are trying to establish a close relationship with will have to see the parts of you that you don't think are worthy, the parts that cause you pain. When it comes to establishing a healthy, intimate relationship, the parts of you that you would typically try to conceal would be what you would want to expose. When you show someone the pieces of you that you hide from others, you are saying, I trust you more than anyone else. Until you can open up to someone, you don't truly trust them. If you can't trust a person enough to give them the real version of you, you are wasting your time and theirs. Real intimacy requires vulnerability.

Vulnerability

Merriam Webster defines vulnerability as the capability of being physically or emotionally wounded, open to attack or damage. I believe that vulnerability is one of the biggest reasons it's hard for humans to establish intimate relationships with each other and with God. We are so afraid of being hurt that we hide our true selves from the world and God. Fearing vulnerability has been passed down through the generations from Adam and Eve. After they ate from the forbidden tree, they physically hid from God because they were afraid of what would happen (Genesis 3:8-10). Before they ate the fruit, they were both naked and felt no shame (Genesis 2:25). One definition for the word naked is to be without covering or disguise. I believe God used their nakedness as a metaphor for intimacy and vulnerability. Being naked, metaphorically speaking, means that you are exposed. There's nothing covering your imperfections, and there's nothing you can hide. Adam and Eve had no reason to protect themselves before eating the fruit. They were completely comfortable with each other, and they didn't care how they appeared. They never even knew what being naked was until the serpent slithered his way in. After they disobeyed God, their eyes were opened, and everything changed. When Adam and Eve realized they were naked, they were ashamed, so they covered themselves and hid their bodies from each other, then they hid from God (Genesis 3:7-8). Until sin showed up, insecurity didn't exist. Adam and Eve had the courage to show their true selves.

When they sinned, not only did they realize their bodies were exposed, but Adam exposed his wife as well. God asked Adam if he ate from the tree that He told them not to eat from, and Adam exposed his wife by basically saying it's all her fault (Genesis 3:12). I can only imagine the look on Eve's face. The only person you care about just threw you under the bus! I believe this is the moment when the struggle with being vulnerable began.

Like Adam and Eve, we have a problem exposing our true selves to each other and God. We act like God has no clue who we are, even though He created us. And we are arrogant enough to believe that we can fool the creator of the universe. When you try to hide the real you from God, you tell Him that you don't trust Him, and it's impossible to have a healthy relationship with someone you don't trust. Hebrews 4:13 (NLT) says, "Nothing in all creation is hidden from God. Everything is naked and exposed before his eyes." He already saw you before you tried to put that holy filter on this morning. Keeping your authentic self from God does nothing but prolong your blessing. Your Heavenly Father already knows what's going on. He just wants you to tell Him so that you can admit whether you trust Him or not.

You don't have to be afraid of being intimate with God because He loves you, and He will never do anything to hurt you. There's no sin too great that will cause God to turn his back on you. His son died so that we could be forgiven. Everything that we have ever done that disappointed God has been thrown into the sea of forgetfulness. Remember, our Daddy God is not like man. We have to look at Him as the supreme being that He is. How would God benefit from lying on us, laughing at us, abusing our feelings, or mistreating us? God is Alpha and Omega, and all things fall subject to Him, so what would be the point of using our imperfections against us? It's not like He has a social circle to sit and gossip with. God's not sitting on His throne, laughing, and telling the angels about our shortcomings. He created our lives from beginning to end. He's seen everything we've done and will do before we were even a thought. So suck it up, and be honest with your Heavenly Father. The worst thing that could happen is you get closer to Him.

People fear vulnerability because they don't want their weaknesses exposed. Someone who doesn't want their weaknesses exposed will put up a defense to protect themselves from harm. Look at how defensive Adam got when God questioned him; he blamed it all on "the woman God gave him (Genesis 3:12)." He never took responsibility for his part, even though God initially talked to Adam when he said He didn't want them to eat the fruit (Genesis 2:16-17). I believe that although Eve was meant to be Adam's help, Satan used her as Adam's weakness. He knew how much Adam trusted Eve, and he used her to do his bidding.

Fortunately for us, exposing our weaknesses to God will work better in our favor than hiding them. Weakness is a part of His plan. He gives us all weaknesses, so we would have to rely on Him to be successful. God also allows us to be weak in certain areas to keep us close to Him.

Let's take a look at 2 Corinthians 12:7-10 in the Message Bible:

"...so I wouldn't get a big head, I was given the gift of a handicap to keep me in constant touch with my limitations. Satan's angel did his best to get me down; what he in fact did was push me to my knees. No danger then of walking around high and mighty! At first I didn't think of it as a gift, and begged God to remove it. Three times I did that, and then he told me, 'My grace is enough; it's all you need. My strength comes into its own in your weakness'. ...I quit focusing on the handicap and began appreciating the gift. It was a case of Christ's strength moving in on my weakness. Now I take limitations in stride, and with good cheer, these limitations that cut me down to size—abuse, accidents, opposition, bad breaks. I just let Christ take over! And so the weaker I get, the stronger I become."

You have to remember that God doesn't want us to think we gained our success on our own, so He has to make sure we recognize that it's His strength that causes us to be successful. Your weaknesses were designed to force you to seek God's strength so that you can overcome whatever is standing in your way. God works in you and through you when you are weak, so His will can be accomplished (Phillipians 2:13). Therefore, there is no need to fear being vulnerable with your Heavenly Father because weakness ultimately leads to your success.

Don't Fear Rejection

One of the main things that stop people from having intimate relationships is their fear of being rejected by someone they desire. The fear of rejection can hold you back from letting your guard down and allowing someone to see who you truly are. When you fear rejection, you don't take chances, which could hold you back from many experiences, and you miss out on great things.

When it comes to God, you will never have to put in more effort or feel like he is rejecting you. Jeremiah 29:13 (ESV) says, "You will seek me and find me when you seek me with all your heart." If you desire a relationship with God, He will be with you. You don't have to worry about trying to get Him to like you or doing what you think will make Him like you. God said if you want me, you got me, no questions asked. The best thing about being in a relationship with God is that God loved us first (1 John 4:19), and He will always desire us to be with Him. He desired, and loved us before we were even born. He even said it in Jeremiah 31:3 (NIV), "I have loved you with an everlasting love." That means God has loved us and will continue to love us until the end of time. You can do absolutely nothing that will make God stop loving you. Nothing can happen that will cause God to lose His desire for you. No matter what you do, you will never be powerful enough to change God's mind about you. I am essentially saying the same thing three different ways, because I want you to see how important this is. God will love you forever, and He will want you always. God will never leave you, and He will never turn his back on you Hebrews 13:5).

God loves you so much, He allows you to reject Him daily with your behavior (disobedience, sin, etc....), and He still loves and protects you. Look at it like this, every time you disobey what God asked you to do, whether you break a commandment or you defy His specific instruction for your life, you are rejecting God. It could be something as simple as not putting the dishes away after your mother asked since God told us to obey our parents (Exodus 6:1-3). God has given us the world. The least we can do is actively try to keep his commandments. Yes, there will be times when we fall short, but as long as we ask for forgiveness, are making an effort to change our behavior, and follow His instructions, we're good.

Chapter 4 Journaling Questions

What can you do to show God that you desire Him?

Is there any part of you that you are trying to hide from God? If so, what are you hiding from Him?

Is there anything that you are insecure about? If so, what are your insecurities?

"Dear Heavenly Father, you are an all-knowing and an all-powerful God. Lord, thank you for loving me more than I will ever be able to comprehend. I thank you for loving me so much that you gave your only son so that I can be able to spend eternity with you. Father, I ask that you increase my desire to know you better by reading your word, give me a desire to serve you, and give me a desire to spend more time speaking and listening to you. Your word says that you will give me the desires of my heart, and I know that if I am walking in your will for my life, the desires in my heart come from you, so I ask that you manifest those desires. I also ask that you take away from me every desire that I have that does not line up with the purpose you have for me. Father, I thirst for you. Help me understand the kind of relationship you desire from me right now. I ask that you help me see myself the way You see me. I want to be the woman You predestined me to be, and the only way that I can do that is by standing in the authority you have given me through your Son Jesus Christ. Your word says that I am the head and not the tail, above only and not beneath and I pray that I will no longer be bound by my insecurities. I want to live a free life. I no longer want my insecurities to stop me from being who you created me to be. I know that I have been fearfully and wonderfully made and the word that you have placed over my life will come to pass. I surrender myself to you. I love you, Daddy, thank you for everything, Amen."

5

~

Choose Wisely

Freewill

When God created you, He didn't give you a script or a program that you have to follow. Yes, you have the Bible that provides you with instruction, but there's nothing set in place that makes you do what is instructed. No one in the Heavenlies is controlling you, making you move, act, or speak. Instead, God gave you the ability to make choices on your own. Every choice that you make results in some consequence. That consequence can be good or bad, but because you can decide your fate, you have to accept whatever happens due to the choices you make. Although God has a desired plan for your life, what happens in your life is ultimately up to you. Deuteronomy 30:19-20 (ESV) explains it like this:

"I call heaven and earth to witness against you today, that I have set before you life and death, blessing and curse. Therefore choose life, that you and your offspring may live, loving the Lord your God, obeying his voice and holding fast to him, for he is your life and length of days, that you may dwell in the land that the Lord swore to your fathers, to Abraham, to Isaac, and to Jacob, to give them."

God loves you so much; He gives you the freedom to choose Him or not. He doesn't force you to serve Him; He gives you a choice. Whatever choice you make, you have to be willing to accept what comes with that choice. The scripture shows that you only have two options: life or death. Take that literally. If you choose God, there's life in Him, but if you don't choose God, you automatically accept the way that leads to death. Death, in this context, has the same meaning as it did with Adam and Eve. It means to be without the presence of God in your life.

The choices you make can bring you closer to God or cause you to walk away from His presence. When you choose to do what you want to do instead of what God is asking you to do, you are not choosing the way that leads to eternal life with Him. So if you're not choosing life in Him by being obedient, then you are choosing to be without God's presence. God will not protect you from Satan's attack when you make that choice. It's not that He doesn't want to protect you or that He's not able to. He's honoring the choice you made. Your choice to consistently disobey God's instruction causes you to walk out of the presence of God, leaving you open for Satan to bring destruction into your life.

Let's take a look at Psalm 91, which is known as the Psalm of protection. Moses did a great job explaining how God's protection works. The Psalm starts by depicting God's presence as a shadow. Think about how shadows work. If you walk into a tree's shadow, you are in the shade and protected from the sun. Eventually, if you keep walking, you will walk out of the shadow, and the tree will no longer shield you from the sun. God's presence works the same way. When you choose to follow God's instruction, you are choosing to be under His shadow. As long as you follow Him, you are in His shadow, and He will protect you. However, once you decide to disobey His instructions, He will no longer shield you from danger because you chose to walk out of His shadow of protection. Isaiah 54:17 (NLT) tells us,

> "But in that coming day, no weapon turned against you will succeed. You will silence every voice raised up to accuse you. These benefits are enjoyed by the servants of the Lord; their vindication will come from me. I, the Lord, have spoken!"

Notice the scripture says, "These benefits are enjoyed by the servants of the Lord." A servant is someone who follows their master's instruction. The scripture explains that God will stop weapons from attacking the people who obey His commands.

God's Grace

God's grace is given to people who love Him. Your Heavenly Father understands that you aren't perfect, and you will fall victim to temptation sometimes, so God extends grace to you so that He can save you from sin (Romans 6:14). When God extends grace to you, it means that He understands that sometimes things can be challenging, and because He loves you, He allows you to make mistakes without turning His back on you. God's extension of grace saves you from many of the consequences that come from disobedience. Grace also teaches you to walk away from sin and live a life that pleases God. The English Standard Version of Titus 2:11-12 says,

"For the grace of God has appeared, bringing salvation for all people, training us to renounce ungodliness and worldly passions, and to live self-controlled, upright, and godly lives in the present age..."

This verse shows that grace trains us to renounce ungodliness and worldly passions. Sin is a part of human nature, and you have to learn how to live a Godly life. No matter who you are, there will be times when you struggle with living a Godly life. However, if you embrace the grace that God extends to you from the resurrection of His son Jesus Christ, you can learn how to have self-control and live a life that satisfies God, even in a world filled with temptation.

Even though you will stumble, God will not let the ones who love Him fall (Psalm 37:23-24). Keep in mind there's a difference between stumbling and blatantly disobeying. Stumbling and disobeying have two different attitudes behind them. People who stumble are trying to do right but make a mistake. In the book of James, we can see that grace is given to those who are humble about their mistakes. James 4:6-10 (NLT) says,

"And he gives grace generously. As the Scriptures say, 'God opposes the proud but gives grace to the humble.' So hum- ble yourselves before God. Resist the devil, and he will flee from you. Come close to God, and God will come close to you. Wash your hands, you sinners; purify your hearts, for your loyalty is divided between God and the world. Let there be tears for what you have done. Let there be sorrow and deep grief. Let there be sadness instead of laughter, and gloom instead of joy. Humble yourselves before the Lord, and he will lift you up in honor."

Your actions become sinful when you are conscious of your wrongdoing, and you do it anyway (James 4:17). The word says in 2 Corinthians 7:9-10 (NLT),

> "...the pain caused you to repent and change your ways. It was the kind of sorrow God wants his people to have... For the kind of sorrow God wants us to experience leads us away from sin and results in salvation. There's no regret for that kind of sorrow. But worldly sorrow, which lacks repentance, results in spiritual death."

When you don't feel guilty about disobeying God, then you have willingly walked out of God's presence.

Don't Be Mad

King Solomon explained the importance of our choices in Proverbs 14. I prefer the New Living Translation for this particular passage because of its descriptiveness. Solomon explains what happens when a person follows God's instruction versus someone who chooses their own path. In verse two, He makes it very clear what happens, "Those who follow the right path fear the Lord; those who take the wrong path despise him."

If you continue reading Proverbs 14, you will find many examples of what happens when you choose your own will over God's. For instance, verse 11 says, "The house of the wicked will be destroyed, but the tent of the godly will flourish." And verse 14 explains that backsliders (people who know God but walk away from Him) get what they deserve, and good people receive their reward. When you choose not to follow God's instruction, you are putting yourself in harm's way. When you consistently make choices contrary to God's will for your life you cause God to remove His hand of protection from your life. God can not perform something contrary to His word, so He is not allowed to protect you from the foolish choices He told you not to make.

Under no circumstance do you have the right to be mad at God when your decisions result in something you do not like. For example, if you choose to have unprotected, premarital sex with somebody's raggedy son, you can't be mad when your baby daddy is trash. God never told you to sleep with that loser. Your body belongs to God, and He intended for you to give it to your husband only. Sex outside of marriage is stepping outside of God's will for your life. So, whatever happens, good or bad, you have to accept that consequence.

To be clear, I am not shaming people who have premarital sex. I'm simply using it as an example to show our choices go far beyond the present moment. Premarital sex is one of the best examples to show how significant your choices are. One moment, whether you enjoyed it or not, can change the entire course of your life. You have to look at the bigger picture. If I do this, will my Daddy God be pleased, or am I choosing to step out of His shadow of protection? And if I do decide to step out of God's will for my life, am I willing to accept whatever happens as a result? As I said earlier, there are only two choices: life - God's blessings and protection or death - life without God's protection and blessing. The choice is yours, but as for me and my house, we will serve the Lord (Joshua 24:15).

Surrender

To protect ourselves from hurt feelings, we tend to enter into relationships swinging every weapon we have, and on top of that, we put up walls that seem impossible to get through. Although God is a supreme being who can tear down any barriers you put up, He's not going to intrude. Like I said before, He's a gentleman. Surrender has to be a conscious decision that you make. When you surrender yourself to someone in a natural relationship, you freely give yourself to that person.

Surrendering to someone is not an easy task at all. It takes maximum effort. It's one of the hardest parts of being in a relationship with someone, and if you think about it, it should be hard. Everyone does not deserve your surrender. Everyone is not worthy of having that much access to you or power over you. When you surrender yourself to someone, you say that you belong to that person, and giving someone that much power could be dangerous.

Fortunately, there's no risk or danger involved in surrendering to God. When you surrender to God, you are saying, "Ok God, I belong to you, and whatever you want for me, I'm ok with it because I know that you know what's best for my life." The short version is, "Jesus take the wheel!" When you choose to follow God, it means that you are choosing His will for your life over your own. In Luke 9:23, Jesus told the crowd that if you choose to follow Him, you have to let Him lead. The Message version says, "You're not in the driver's seat I am."

Many scriptures let us know that God knew us and had plans for us before we were formed in our mother's womb (Jeremiah 1:5, Jeremiah 29:11-14, Ephesians 2:10, Isaiah 44:2, Psalm 139:16). It is our job to surrender to those plans. We weren't placed on this earth to follow our selfish plan. God has plans for you, and your success in life is attached to those plans. It is your responsibility to find out what those plans are and the only way you can do that is by letting God know that you are going to do what He's asking of you, no matter what the assignment may be. Although it's not an easy task, giving Jesus the wheel will be the best decision you have ever made.

When I was a kid, I had a huge collection of Barbies. My playroom was filled with Barbie houses, cars, career settings, and a high school. I even had a storage case that was the home to hundreds of outfits and accessories. I knew every Barbie doll by name, and they all had their own personalities, careers, style, cars, homes, etc. Each storyline was unique, and each Barbie doll had its own thing going on. Not one doll was the same, not even when someone purchased a Barbie for me that I already had. She got a new name and personality. I was the creator of my pink universe. I knew every detail about my creations and their storylines. As their creator, I had a plan for their lives, and they were helpless without me. The same thing is true for you and God. God is your creator, and He knows every little detail about your life, and He created your storyline.

Our heavenly Father would love for you to follow His plan for the life He gave you, but He's not going to make you do anything. The difference between you and my Barbies is that God gave you free will. You have a choice to follow his storyline or create your own. My Barbies had to do what I told them to because I was moving them, and they were lifeless objects. You, on the other hand, have the freedom of choice.

When you choose to take your life into your own hands, you risk messing it up. Be honest with yourself. You have no idea what you're doing when it comes to life in general. I've technically been an adult for 15 years now, and I can honestly say I have no clue what I'm doing. Adulting is the hardest! It seemed so cool to be a grown-up when I was a kid. Nobody told me that no one knows what they're doing, and you spend the majority of your time trying to figure things out. There's no instruction manual, and everything changes as soon as you think you know what's going on. Things are more manageable if you have a good parent who can help you out a little, but even their instruction isn't always the best. To surrender to God, you have to be willing to completely depend on His instruction and stop trying to do things your way. Isaiah 30:15-18 (MSG) says,

"God, the Master, The Holy of Israel, has this solemn counsel:
"Your salvation requires you to turn back to me and stop your silly

efforts to save yourselves. Your strength will come from settling down in complete dependence on me— The very thing you've been unwilling to do... He's waiting around to be gracious to you. He's gathering strength to show mercy to you. God takes the time to do everything right—everything. Those who wait around for him are the lucky ones."

In order to surrender in any situation, you have to trust that whatever, or whoever you are surrendering to will not lead you into something negative. Jeremiah 29:11 tells us that God knows the plans He has for us and those plans will not cause us harm and they are not evil plans. The plans that God has for us are to give us a future with Him as well as hope. Hope can be defined as a feeling of expectation and desire, and a feeling of trust. If God has plans to give us hope, which is a feeling of trust, then He can't also have plans to hurt us or cause us harm because that will contradict who He is and will lead to us not trusting Him. Since God is the truth (John 14:6), He cannot lie (Numbers 23:19). So when He says that His plans are going to bring you a future and a hope, He means it.

Chapter 5 Journaling Questions

Do you think that true surrender is hard? If so, Why?

Have you surrendered everything to God? If not, what are you holding back from him and why?

"Dear Heavenly Father, you are the creator of all things. You created my beginning and my ending before I was even born. You gave me every gift and unique talent I have, and I thank you for creating me. Thank you for giving me a choice to spend eternity with you or do my own thing. Father, I ask that you help me surrender my will to you and live a life that pleases you. I ask that you show me which way to go and what to do to stay on the path you have for me. I don't want to disappoint you. I want to make you proud of your daughter. Please forgive me for the choices that I have made that were not pleasing to you. Please help me be more obedient and recognize that each day I wake up, I belong to you, and I represent you. I love you, Daddy. Thank you for everything, Amen."

6

⌇

Talk to God

Communication is the act of making yourself understood. It's how you express your thoughts, opinions, ideas, and desires. Communication helps you develop your relationship and connect on a deeper level. I can't say that I know my husband if I never speak or listen to him. How do I know his likes or dislikes, and how would I have known his intentions if I had never talked to him? The same thing applies to your relationship with God. How can you say that you know Him if you don't communicate with Him? How will you know God's plan for your life if you don't ask Him?

God gave you the ability to pray so you can talk to Him. To effectively communicate with God, you must understand that prayer is not about using the "right" words. Anyone can pray. You don't have to sound like you're the honorable Reverend Dr. Bishop. Talk to your Heavenly Father like you usually talk to someone you love. I've noticed that when I try to sound holy, I am focusing more on the technique instead of being intimate with my Heavenly Father. I have to give room for my heart to speak directly with God. When I allow what's going on in my heart to flow out, I feel more connected to God's Spirit. I feel like the world has stopped so that He can listen to me. You don't have to try to impress God with your prayers. He already thinks you're incredible; you're His creation. Prayer is having a meaningful conversation with God. The relationship you have with Him is about the two of you, and He wants to know your heart.

When we are having a difficult time, we tend to call our friends or post on social media when, in reality, there's not much they can do for us. We know that they can't fix whatever is bothering us, but most of the time, we just like sympathy. Instead of reaching out to people to feel sorry for us, we have a Heavenly Father waiting for us to talk to Him first. Then, God will provide you with guidance guaranteed to work and genuine comfort. Can you always count on your friends to do the same? Since God is eternal, and He knows our end before our beginning, wouldn't it make sense to ask our creator for help instead of asking a fellow creation for help? Especially when our friends have problems of their own to deal with.

Ephesians 6:18 talks about praying at all times and staying alert and persistent. We should talk to God about EV-VER-RY-THING!! Prayer is sharing our thoughts, heart's desires, dreams, and how we feel with our Heavenly Father. To pray correctly, you have to turn off the filter and express yourself. Want to know a secret? When you share your innermost, heartfelt secrets and desires with God, you never have to worry about Him telling anyone. God won't be upset with you, and He won't make you feel ashamed or judged. Your secrets are safe with Him. The only thing God wants from you in return is love.

How strong would your connection with your significant other be if you never had a heartfelt compliment to give them and all you did was complain? What if you only made requests and never shared your heart with them? Do you think they would be happy with you? So why do we believe we can act like that with the one who created us? God didn't create us so He could please us. We were created to please God. Please means to be happy and satisfied. Although 1 John 3:22 says that God will give us what we ask for, do you think God is satisfied and happy when we don't seek a deeper relationship with Him? How about when we don't take time to love on Him or pour our hearts out to Him? There should always be a moment in your day when you say, "Lord, I love you," without bombarding him with a million and twelve "Lord can you" type statements.

Sometimes people's prayers make me think people think God is a Genie. Their entire prayer is full of demands disguised as requests. God is not a genie. He does not live in a lamp, and you are not entitled to anything. We can't make God do anything that He has not already intended on doing for us. God is in control, so whatever we do receive from Him, He's the one who decided to give it to us.

Your Heavenly Father has no problem giving you the desires of your heart. He says that we should ask Him, in confidence, for what we want, and He will give it to us (Mathew 7:7, John 14:13, 1 John 5:14). Throughout the Bible, we see that God blessed people because of something they did and not just because they asked. For example, Deuteronomy 28 talks about the blessings of the Lord, but the passage begins by saying, "If you faithfully obey the voice of the Lord your God, being careful to do all His commandments...." Obey and Do are both action words, which means you have to take action before the blessing comes. During your prayer time, the action you take is an essential part of your relationship with God.

To get the most out of your prayer time there's a basic format that you should try to follow: Honor, thank, ask. Jesus shows us this format in the Lord's prayer which you can find in Matthew 6:9-13 and Luke 11:2-4. Remember when your friends would want to spend the night, but you had to be the one that asked because you knew what to say? The Lord's prayer is just like that. Jesus showed us how to talk to His dad so that we could get the best outcome.

Jesus tells us to begin prayer by going to God as His child by calling him, Father. The next step is praising Him for who He is to you. Which means complimenting our Father:

"Heavenly Father, you are awesome and I love you so much, there's no one above you..."

Next, God wants to know that you trust him to care for your needs. Your needs include provision, shelter, protection, and direction:

"I thank you for providing for me, and for your hand of protection that is always on me. I thank you for your wisdom and guidance..."

When you pray, you should also ask God to forgive you for doing things that did not please Him and to change your ways so that you do please Him:

"Father forgive me for doing things that are not pleasing to you. Please help me be more aware of the things that break your heart so that I can turn away from them and live a life that pleases you..."

Along with asking for forgiveness for your sins, you also need to let God know that you need his help forgiving the people who hurt you:

"Please help me forgive the people that hurt me and show me how you want me to pray for them..."

Those were just some of the main ingredients of an effective prayer. There's no rule saying that this is the only way to pray. As long as you cover these basics, you're on the right track. The great part about communicating with God is that you don't even have to know what to say all the time. When you love God, He gives you His Spirit, and since a part of Him is in You, He can communicate directly with the Spirit He placed inside of you. Romans 8:26-27 (ESV) says,

> "The Spirit helps us in our weakness. For we do not know what to pray for as we ought, but the Spirit himself intercedes for us with groaning too deep for words. And He who searches hearts knows what is the mind of the Spirit, because the Spirit intercedes for the saints according to the will of God".

There are times when I'm at a loss for words, so instead of running my mouth and repeating things over and over, which God doesn't like anyway (Matthew 6:7, Ecclesiastes 5:2), I look up scriptures that deal with my situation. Speaking God's word back to Him is my favorite way to pray. God created the world with His words, so why not speak His words back to him? The Bible says that God is not a man, so He cannot lie (Numbers 23:19), and since I know that the Bible is full of God's promises and truths, I like to say what the Bible says when I pray. That way, I know that my words have God's power, specific for the situation. After praying the word, which is the sword of the Spirit (Ephesians 6:17), I feel more confident that my situation will change.

When someone asks me to pray for them, I like to pray using God's word for two reasons. Number one, I never want to take God's glory like Herod did (an Angel struck him down, and maggots ate him, (Acts 12:22-23)). Second, I can text someone a prayer filled with the word of God, and when they read it, they're also speaking the word over their life.

I have a list of scriptures that I read every morning that helps me get ready for the day, and I have a separate set that I read at night. Since I've been praying using those scriptures, I noticed that my confidence, peace, and health have increased, and my anxiety and disobedience have decreased. If you want to create your own lists of scriptures, I suggest you start reading through Psalm and Proverbs because they are full of God's promises. As you read through those books, highlight the different promises you want to claim for your life. The more you read your Bible, the more the Spirit will begin to show you scriptures that you can read for every situation you face. Pick out a few and add them to your daily scriptures. Next, think about the things that concern you most and search online for scriptures for whatever the topic is (i.e., scriptures for anxiety, scriptures for depression, scriptures for joy, etc.) and add those to the list. Speaking and reading God's word isn't just our way of communicating with Him but His Spirit uses it to communicate with us. We will explore that more in the next chapter.

Chapter 6 Journaling Questions

On a scale from 1-10, How well have you communicated with God lately? (1 non-existent, 10 excellent)

How can you improve if it's not where you would like it to be?

"Dear Heavenly Father, you are so full of love, and I thank you for loving me enough to give me a way of communicating with you. Thank you for giving me the ability to speak with you through prayer. Father, I ask that you help me be more eager to spend time with you. I pray that my excitement to tell you about my day, my desires, and my dreams grow daily. I want to look forward to our daddy-daughter time. I ask that you quiet the noise around me and remove all distractions so that I can focus on you alone during our time together. I pray that I become more and more comfortable laying my heart at your feet and receiving your love during our talks. Forgive me for allowing things to get in the way of our time together. I promise that I will work hard on creating time for you daily. I love you, Daddy. Thank you for everything, Amen."

7

～

Listen for God

Communication is two-fold, meaning there are two parts to it. You not only have to be willing to speak, but you also have to be willing to actively listen. Actively listening is when you are quiet and focusing on what the other person is trying to say. A lot of times, people only pretend to listen during a conversation. Most of the time, when a person listens, they're thinking about their next response. When you're not quietly focusing on the message that the other person is trying to communicate, you are not actively listening; you're just hearing, waiting for your turn to speak.

Communication isn't just two-fold in the natural, but it is also two-fold in the spiritual. Prayer is a conversation with God. You have to be willing to listen for God's voice; however He chooses to speak to you. There were only a few times in the Bible that God spoke audibly to His people. Today, you may never hear God audibly speaking directly to you like he did in biblical times because He gave us other ways to hear Him. We hear God through His Son Jesus Christ, His written Word, His Spirit, and through prayer. God can also use nature and His creations, other believers, music, and our circumstances or experiences. The fact of the matter is, if God needs to tell you something, He will do whatever it takes to get His point across. Below, I will highlight how God chooses to speak to His people.

Jesus Christ

Hebrews 1:2 says, "And now in these final days, He has spoken to us through His Son. God promised everything to the Son as an inheritance, and through the Son, he created the Universe." Jesus was sent to Earth to be the middleman between us and our Heavenly Father (1 Timothy 2:5). I know parents aren't supposed to have favorites, but we all know which one we would send to get our parents to say yes to our request. Consider Jesus our Heavenly Father's favorite child. He's the one we talk to so He can go to Daddy and come back and tell us what He said. Since we know that Jesus is the favorite, it's only right for us to listen to Him. We also know that Jesus is God's literal right-hand man (Matthew 26:64), so what He says will not lead us astray. Instead, it will direct us right to the Father. So when you read your Bible, pay close attention to what Jesus said because it's a message from our Father.

God's Spirit, His Written Word & Prayer

The Spirit that God placed inside of you might be the most valuable thing about you, so you need to know what it's about. John 14:26 describes the Holy Spirit as the helper that our Heavenly Father sent in Jesus' name. The Holy Spirit is responsible for teaching you everything and helping you remember what your Heavenly Father has spoken to you through His written word or a word given directly to you. Ephesians 6:17 tells us that the word of God (the scriptures in the Bible) is the sword of the Holy Spirit, so we have to read our Bible.

The Holy Spirit can't be our helper if we don't give Him something to fight with. Imagine being sent to war with no weapon. When you don't spend time reading and retaining the information laid out for you in the Bible, you are sending your Spirit into battle unarmed. We don't read our Bibles but wonder why we don't see any movement in our situations. Without the proper preparation, your Spirit can't bring back to your remembrance what you need when it's time to fight. For example, God might lead you to speak to someone about something important, and right before it's time to speak, you get fearful. In this instance, the Holy Spirit should be able to bring to your memory a version of scripture that deals with fear. Maybe something like Philippians 4:6-7 (NLT),

"Don't worry about anything; instead, pray about everything. Tell God what you need, and thank him for all he has done. Then you will experience God's peace, which exceeds anything we can understand. His peace will guard your hearts and minds as you live in Christ Jesus."

If you're able to bring a scripture like this to your mind, the Spirit will not only address your fear; He will also give you direction. "Don't worry, tell God what you need, thank God, and live in Christ Jesus." Along with receiving guidance, you also received a promise, "You will experience God's peace, and it will guard your hearts and minds."

It's important to read God's word because then your Spirit and you will speak the same language as God. By the law that God established, He has to respond to His word, so if your Spirit speaks the word, God has to do whatever His word said according to Corinthians 1:20-22 (MSG),

"Whatever God has promised gets stamped with the Yes of Jesus. In him, this is what we preach and pray, the great Amen, God's Yes and our Yes together, gloriously evident. God affirms us, making us a sure thing in Christ, putting his Yes within us. By his Spirit he has stamped us with his eternal pledge—a sure beginning of what he is destined to complete."

I don't suggest focusing on the exact wording of the scripture because I don't expect you to memorize every scripture you'll need word for word. As long as you know the basic meaning of the scripture, you can speak like God speaks. The more you read the scriptures, the easier it will be for you to bring them back to your memory as needed. I have a list of scriptures that I read daily that focus on particular areas in my life, so when I need to call on a scripture that will address a specific area, I can refer to one of those. The more I read them, the more they are hidden in my heart, and the easier it is for me to bring them to mind when needed.

When you speak like God speaks, it's also easier for you to hear what He is trying to say to you. Being in tune with His Spirit that lives inside of you is the biggest cheat code in the Universe. God is the creator of the entire Universe. He has written every version of your story possible. Everything that is ever going to happen in your life, God already knows about it. Since you have access to the Spirit in Him, you have access to your future through the Holy Spirit. If the Holy Spirit knows what God knows, the best thing you can do for your future is to allow His Spirit to guide you.

"When the Spirit of truth comes, he will guide you into all the truth, for he will not speak on his own authority, but whatever he hears he will speak, and he will declare to you the things that are to come" - John 16:3, ESV.

Being led by the Spirit isn't as spooky as you might think. Have you ever been involved in a situation, and suddenly you don't feel right. There might be an uneasiness in your stomach or something else that lets you know that something's not right. Some people say it's your woman's intuition or an ancestor, but those of us that know Jesus know that's His Spirit warning you. If you pay more attention to those moments, you will begin to notice that your Spirit is nudging you. Not only does your Spirit provide warning, but there's also a promise to provide a way out of trouble (1 Corinthians 10:13). If you allow yourself to be led by the Holy Spirit, you can avoid the roadblocks and misdirections in life. I know this spiritual stuff needs more explanation, and I promise that we will revisit this in more detail later in the chapters about Blessing Patterns, Sin Patterns, and Strongholds.

Other Believers

Another way that we can hear God is through other believers. All of God's children have received spiritual gifts, and the Bible says that if you have a spiritual gift to speak, only speak what God says (1 Peter 4:10-11). In Hosea 12:10, God says, "I spoke to the prophets, gave them many visions and told parables through them," and in 1 Corinthians 14:3, we see that the ones who God uses to speak to His people, speak to build up, to encourage and to consult. Although it's possible to hear God through other believers, it's important to pay attention to what people say God is saying to you or about you. Everyone does not speak for God. 1 John 4 warns us of false prophets (people who speak the opposite of what God speaks and say they speak for God). Everyone who you hear God from is not a prophet. Sometimes the voice of God might come through a parent, a teacher, a friend, or a co-worker. God can use anyone to speak to you. In Numbers 22:28, He used a Donkey to talk.

Music

For many of us, music is a part of our daily lives. We have smart speakers and smartphones that can play almost any song we can think of. Many of us use music as a retreat. If you're anything like me, you can find yourself lost in the music. Because of my relationship with music, I pay close attention to the words I allow to enter my ears. When I seek guidance or comfort for a particular situation, I listen to songs that contain the power of God's word. Christian & Gospel artists who write what the word says are giving you a way to hide God's word in your heart so your Spirit can use it to speak to you when needed. Sometimes you might be waiting to hear from God, and then a particular song pops in your head. The next time that happens, ask God to open your ears to hear whatever He is trying to say to you as you listen to the song. Also, if you're going through a troubling situation, play some praise and worship music. The Bible says that praise silences the enemy and all that oppose you (Psalm 8:2).

Remember that if God can speak to you through music, so can the one he intended to be the worship leader of Heaven, Lucifer (Satan's angel name). In Ezekiel 28:13, God said that Lucifer was perfect and beautiful, and the workmanship of His timbrels and pipes (tambourines and horned instruments) was prepared for him the day he was created. This shows us that when Lucifer was in Heaven, God's will for him was to have some kind of authority over the music in Heaven. Just because he got kicked out of Heaven does not mean he lost all access to music. He may not be in charge of Heaven's music, but God made him the ruler of this world (John 12:31), so he still has some authority over the world's music. The way he's described in the Message version and the New King James version of Ezekiel 28:13 leads me to believe that God had big plans for him. This also leads me to believe that God and Satan both know the importance of music. The Bible says that Lucifer's body was made out of every precious stone (Ezekiel 28:13), and in the book Rebirth of Music, LaMar Boschman writes that Lucifer's body had pipes and tambourines built right into him. If the ministry of music was not important, I doubt God would've taken his time crafting such a beautiful creature.

How Do I Know I'm Hearing God?

When it comes to listening in the natural, I consider myself to be pretty awesome at it, but I am still trying to master that skill in the spiritual. The difficulty that many people have when listening for God's voice is that they are confused about whether or not they are hearing from God. Sometimes I question whether I heard God or did I just hear myself in my mind. So I can hear His voice, most of the time, I write in a prayer journal. I noticed that writing things down organizes my thoughts and helps me ignore the rest of the random nonsense floating around my mind. I believe that the enemy tries to flood my mind with tons of thoughts while I'm trying to pray so that He can get me sidetracked. To combat the slick attack, I ask God to clear my mind of all distractions and open my ears so that I may hear Him clearly, however He chooses to speak.

Another way that has helped me understand whether it's God or me is by dissecting what I heard or felt. Whatever I hear or feel God is saying, I run it against God's attributes and promises that I have found in scriptures like 1 John 4:2-3 suggests we do. If what I heard does not contradict God's attributes or promises, I move forward, trusting that it is Him. If there is even just a slight contradiction, I dismiss the thought. When I asked God how I know when he's speaking to me, I was reminded that intimacy is essential. I was told to be alert and watch His patterns so I can know Him when I see Him.

Chapter 7 Journaling Questions

On a scale from 1-10, How well are you listening for God's voice? (1 not listening, 10 excellent listener)

What do you think is stopping you from hearing His voice? What can you do to improve?

"Dear Heavenly Father, you are a great and powerful God. Everything on Earth falls subject to you. Thank you for your written word that gives me instruction, shows me your promises and gives me hope. I ask that you give me a desire to study your word so that I can use your word when I need to. I thank you for the many ways you chose to speak to me. I ask that you open my ears so I can hear you and open my heart to receive what you're saying to me. Father, I ask that you quiet my thoughts when I'm trying to hear from you. I want to give you my undivided attention because you deserve it. I ask that you show me the people you have placed in my life who I can trust to speak your word in my life. If people around me intentionally speak things contrary to your word, please let me recognize it and not take their words to heart. I love you, Daddy. Thank you for everything, Amen."

8

⁓

Blessing & Sin Patterns

Every once in a while, you have to slow things down and re-read your story. Re-reading your story means that you are taking time to reflect on what has happened in your life. You should always be aware of your individual story because you can find answers for your future by finding the patterns in your past. When you begin to recognize the patterns of behavior in your life, you will see your story and the world differently. By identifying those patterns, you can set expectations, connect experiences and behaviors, and see the bigger picture. Vanessa Miemis, author of the blog, *Emergent by Design*, had this to say about the importance of patterns:

"The ability to spot existing or emerging patterns is one of the most (if not the most) critical skills in intelligent decision making, though we're mostly unaware that we do it all the time. Combining past experience, intuition, and common sense, the ability to recognize patterns gives us the ability to predict what will happen next with some degree of accuracy. The better able we are to predict what will happen, the more intelligent we become."

When you make yourself more aware of the patterns in your life, you will be more prepared for action. For example, if your brother is always pulling the chair from underneath you, you'll start to look behind you before you sit down to prevent yourself from hitting your butt on the floor. Being aware of what has happened before gives you insight into how things may go in the future. Take a moment to look back at your life. You have experienced a series of victorious moments, and you have also experienced a series of moments that did not make your Father in heaven or yourself too pleased. I like to refer to these moments as part of your blessing and sin patterns. Blessing and sin patterns help us recognize how God is moving in our lives and how busy the devil is being.

As Christians, sometimes we focus on only the "good" part of Christianity, the blessings. We rejoice every time we feel like God is blessing us. Part of life is embracing both the negative and the positive things that happen to you to appreciate your experiences and allow those experiences to shape you. There isn't one person in this world that has not had both good and bad experiences. It's part of the human struggle of good versus evil.

Good and Evil/Light and Darkness have been going back and forth in the lives of humans since Genesis. At the beginning of creation, God made the first move on darkness by speaking light into existence (Genesis 1:3). When God created vegetation, animals, humans, and everything else and said it was all good (Genesis 1:20 - 31), Satan counter-attacked and tried to separate man from God (Genesis 3). Satan brought sin into Eve's life, establishing the blessing and sin pattern in human beings. Satan temporarily interrupted the blessings that God had laid out for Adam and Eve by enticing Eve to take from the tree of life God told them not to eat from. God gave them access to everything except one tree! The enemy tricked Eve into thinking that God was withholding something she needed from her. The truth was, she didn't even need that one piece of fruit. Eve was blessed with so much, but she allowed what she didn't have nor needed to alter her and her family's future.

When we allow ourselves to be led by the sinful desires of this world like Eve, we put our futures at risk. Not only do we put our futures at risk, but we interrupt the plans that God had for us, and now He has to redirect our lives. Adam and Eve's decision to eat the fruit caused them to get kicked out of the garden, separating them from the presence of God (Genesis 3:23). God had plans for them. He intended for them to kick it with Him in the garden for as long as He desired for them to be there. God's number one desire is for his children to spend eternity with Him. If we are not close to Him, it's our fault. Our choices cause us to be removed from God's presence. Don't be like Adam and Eve, don't allow sinful desires to take you out of God's presence. Colossians 3:1- 25 explains how a child of God should and shouldn't act. I like the instruction that was given in verses 5 - 8 in the Message bible,

"And that means killing off everything connected with that way of death: sexual promiscuity, impurity, lust, doing whatever you feel like whenever you feel like it, and grab- bing whatever attracts your fancy. That's a life shaped by things and feelings instead of by God. It's because of this kind of thing that God is about to explode in anger. It wasn't long ago that you were doing all that stuff and not knowing any better. But you know better now, so make sure it's all gone for good: bad temper, irritability, mean- ness, profanity, dirty talk."

The Bible tells us that we can not allow our lives to be shaped by things and feelings, but we must allow God to make us who we are. Let's get back to Adam and Eve. God told them what not to do, so that should have been it. Instead, Eve allowed things to distract her from what God said. The Serpent used the fruit to attract her fancy so that He could distract her from what God said. The enemy's mouthpiece is so slick (I think that's a reason why he chose to use such a slimy creature like the Serpent).

Read Genesis 3 in the new Living Translation version so you can see what I mean. Here's an excerpt:

> "The Serpent was the shrewdest of all the wild animals the Lord God had made. One day he asked the woman, "Did God really say you must not eat the fruit from any of the trees in the garden?"
>
> "Of course we may eat fruit from the trees in the garden," the woman replied. "It's only the fruit from the tree in the middle of the garden that we are not allowed to eat. God said, 'You must not eat it or even touch it; if you do, you will die.'"
>
> "You won't die!" the Serpent replied to the woman. "God knows that your eyes will be opened as soon as you eat it, and you will be like God, knowing both good and evil."
>
> The woman was convinced. She saw that the tree was beautiful and its fruit looked delicious, and she wanted the wisdom it would give her..."

Pay close attention to the way that the Serpent repurposed God's words. In the New King James Version of the passage, Eve says, "You shall not eat it, nor shall you touch it, lest you die," and then the Serpent says, "You will not surely die." Satan knew what God meant when God said you would die. The Serpent added, not surely, to the sentence. What seems like something small is actually a big deal. Satan is a liar, but He's the best liar out. He knows how to strategically rephrase what God has said to make you think that everything is ok while leading you away from what God has in mind for you.

Eve knew that God said she was not supposed to eat the fruit. She also knew that God said she would die if she touched the tree. She did not understand what God meant when He said she would die, but I believe the Serpent knew. All of this could've been avoided if Eve had taken a moment to ask God what he meant by, you will die. God was not concerned about a physical death at that time (and I wonder if physical death even existed yet). God is always more concerned about his children dying spiritually than physically. When you die spiritually, that means you no longer get to experience the presence of God and everything that comes with that.

It seemed as if the enemy won for a brief moment, but God counterattacked Satan by blessing Adam and Eve with children. If you read throughout the Bible, you will notice that every time evil seemed like it won, good always came back with a blessing that eventually kicked Satan's butt again. In fact, in Genesis 3:15, God tells the Serpent that Him and Eve's offspring, which is us, will always be actively opposed. Now, look at your life. Do you notice the battle of good and evil that has taken place in your life throughout your story?

Just like in the Bible, you can see the evidence of the good vs. evil pattern in your own life. Try identifying the ways Satan has been busy in your life and the ways that God blesses your life. When Satan is active in your life, he persuades you with temptations that look good, but they are harmful to God's plan. Sin patterns usually have to do with something tempting you to do something that you know does not please God, but you struggle with resisting. You often know that it's a sin, but a voice in your head is helping you justify it. The best way to identify a sin pattern is to be aware of the things that don't please God (you can revisit Colossians 3). You can also pay attention to the things that cause you shame after doing them. For example, someone who struggles with overeating will physically and mentally feel terrible after they've overeaten. They might mentally beat themselves up about the act, or they might be disappointed in themselves. Sin patterns are personal. What might be a struggle for you is not necessarily a struggle for everyone.

The pattern occurs after the act is over, and you decide that you're not going to do it again but eventually do. The longer the pattern takes place, the less shame you will feel, making it harder to recognize or break the pattern, increasing the strength of the stronghold. That is why it is important to identify God and the enemy's patterns in your life. When temptation or sin is present, God has designed it so that we are always provided with an exit (1 Corinthians 10:13). We have to be alert enough to see it. One of my favorite passages of scripture in this season of my life is Matthew 11:28-30 (MSG):

> "Are you tired? Worn out? Burned out on religion? Come to me. Get away with me and you'll recover your life. I'll show you how to take a real rest. Walk with me and work with me—watch how I do it. Learn the unforced rhythms of grace. I won't lay anything heavy or ill-fitting on you. Keep company with me and you'll learn to live freely and lightly."

In the above passage, God explains that He wants you to watch how He works in your life. He wants you to learn *His unforced rhythms of grace*. Rhythm can be defined as a strong, regular, repeated pattern of movement. God's unforced rhythms of grace is a fancy way of saying, learn my strong pattern of goodness, it happens regularly, and I am constantly moving. Your Heavenly Father does not force himself to bless you; he does it because he loves you. He wants you to learn the patterns of his goodness so that you can learn to live a life with less stress. Recognize that God always has your best interest in mind, and He has to make sure that His promises happen.

Chapter 8 Journaling Questions

Take some time to look back over your life, what's one example of the fight between Good and Evil in your life?

What's one thing that you know is a struggle for you that you will make a conscious effort to improve?

"Dear Heavenly Father, you created Heaven and Earth and you created light when there was only darkness. Even though Eve caused us to constantly be at war with the serpent, you sent your Son down to Earth to save us from a lifetime full of sin. I am coming to you as your daughter and I am asking you to meet me here. There are things that I struggle with that I know don't make you proud. (Confess your struggles). I no longer want to struggle with these things because they are holding me back from living an abundant life with you. Because I love you, I want to please you in every area of my life. Please help me be the best version of myself. I love you Daddy, thank you for everything, Amen."

9

~

Strongholds

Before I was married, I did not care too much for monogamy. I thought it was a waste of my time. In college, I technically had a boyfriend, but I left him at home so monogamy was the last thing on my mind. One of the most memorable pieces of advice I ever received was, "Boys are like toilet paper, you sh*t on them and keep it moving." As you can see, the person who told me this was not too fond of monogamy. By offering that advice, and leading by example, they passed their lustful sin pattern along to me. Every time they said, "You're just like me," no matter how they used it, they were unknowingly reinforcing the curse, and for a while, I was just like them.

I cheated on my only official college boyfriend the entire time that I was with him. I didn't set out to cheat, and I definitely didn't cheat to intentionally hurt him. In fact, I despised cheaters because of the pain it caused my entire family, but my lustful desire outweighed whatever feelings I had about cheating. Without me knowing, I had been given a desire that was not a part of God's plan for my life. I wasn't connected enough with Christ to be able to withstand my lustful desires.

I was unable to rely on God's strength to keep me away from sin because I was living outside of His presence. I willingly walked out of God's protective shadow and since I was unprotected, the enemy was allowed to use the advice that I received from someone I trusted for his evil plan. In Acts 13:9-10 Saul, aka Paul, called Satan, the enemy of all that is good and said that he is full of deceit and fraud.

The first time I felt guilty, the second time I felt a little bad, but that third time was the charm. After the third time, I was basically a professional cheater and I was never ever gonna get caught. I lost the guilt and I was officially trapped in the enemy's wicked web. While I was feeding the lustful earthly desire that was passed on to me, I was hurting everyone around me! My roommate had to lie for me, the guy I cheated with caught feelings, and of course when I finally confessed to the boyfriend, he was crushed. The enemy was able to manipulate someone I trusted and use them for his will. That person was supposed to instill Godly principles and wisdom into me, but instead, they allowed Satan to use that moment to pass their sinful pattern down to me.

Although the desire was passed on to me, I also have to take responsibility for my own actions. I could've chosen not to cheat, and there were times that I was able to stop myself, but that didn't happen often. During that time, I was not spending as much time with my Heavenly Father and I was not reading my Bible, so I wasn't feeding myself with things that would've built my Spirit up enough to resist temptation. Instead, I listened to a lot of sexually explicit music while putting myself in environments and situations that I knew I shouldn't have been in. Most times, right before I did something that I knew that I shouldn't have, I felt a slight uneasiness in my stomach.

If I was more conscious of my behavior and of God's Spirit, I would've recognized that uneasiness as a warning. Like I said before, God always gives you a way out of temptation, you just have to pay attention. I thank God that people were praying for me and cutting curses off my life without me even knowing. Satan planned on using the generational sin pattern to destroy me but the prayers of the righteous canceled those plans.

Sin patterns are strongholds that are in your life. The word stronghold refers to something that has been fortified or strengthened to protect against attack. A stronghold can be anything that makes it hard for you to experience everything that God has in store for you. They stop you from knowing the truth about who God is as well as the truth about who you are. The lustful desire that I had was a stronghold that was determined to stop me from living my best life, BUT GOD had other plans and He always causes me to triumph (2 Corinthians 2:14)!

If you don't know it yet, if you believe in Jesus Christ, you automatically have the Spirit of God inside of you, but you are also part flesh. God created man from the dust of the earth, which makes him part flesh (of the world) and then God breathed His (breath of) life into Adam making him part spirit (Genesis 2:7). Being part flesh and part spirit means that you have a constant battle going on inside of you. Once again, the battle of good and evil shows itself. In this instance, good is the Spirit of God that lives inside of you and the evil part is the flesh that is also a part of you. When you hear people say, "they're operating in the flesh," it means that the person is making decisions and doing things that don't please God. In Galatians 5:19-21 there's a list of actions made because a person is allowing their flesh to make their decisions. People who make decisions based on worldly desires, also known as flesh, can not please God (Romans 8:8). Therefore, it is important for you to fight these fleshly desires. Your flesh is trying to hold its ground while the Spirit of God is fighting for dominance. A stronghold basically acts as a reinforced forcefield of protection, that protects your flesh from being overtaken by the Spirit. The Spirit of God came so that you will not allow worldly, sinful desires to control you (Galatians 5:16).

Imagine this, there's a villain who has a secret weapon that can control you; let's call it "The Flesh 5000". As long as The Flesh 5000 remains stronger than the hero in our story's Spirit, humanity is in danger and the villain wins. In order to keep control over humanity, the villain has to keep The Flesh 5000 working at 100%. So, the villain takes the flesh 5000 and hides it in a forcefield-protected chest, locked inside of a heavily guarded room, protected by guards with deadly weapons. He calls all of this protection "Stronghold". The villain hides the weapon behind the stronghold because he thinks that we can't harm his Flesh 5000 because of the stronghold. He's partly right, in our own strength we can't do anything about this situation, but our hero can! God is the only one that can break through the stronghold and bring harm to The Flesh 5000.

In other words, strongholds protect the sinfulness inside of you from being extinguished by God's Spirit that dwells in you. In 2 Corinthians 10:4, Paul tells us to use Godly weapons "to knock down strongholds of human reasoning and to destroy false arguments." In verse 5, Paul goes on to tell the people to destroy every obstacle that stops people from knowing God. Remember the biblical meaning of know means to be intimate with. Sin patterns protect your flesh, they are strongholds that stop you from being intimate with your Heavenly Father so they must be canceled. And because this is a spiritual battle, you have to fight it spiritually.

In my own strength, I was unable to recognize the sinful pattern let alone cancel it. Philippians 2:13 reminds us that God is the one who is working in us, giving us the strength to do what will give Him the most pleasure. Sin does not bring God pleasure, so He has to work in you to fix what's wrong. He's contractually obligated to give you strength to cancel the plans of the enemy, He said so in His word.

Resisting Temptation

Now that I am aware that the enemy usually tempts me in the area of my relationships, I am more alert to anything that may try to destroy my marriage, or any other relationship attached to me. I pay more attention to this area than other areas because my purpose is connected to marriage and relationships. I have been called to educate and counsel marriages and families, so of course the enemy would target that area of my life. This does not mean that I don't struggle with sin in other areas of my life, this is the area that I am most aware of right now. I have realized that my biggest temptations are ones that have the ability to destroy my family as well as my purpose. My calling is connected to promoting healthy marriages and families, what do I look like destroying my marriage by entertaining somebody's son in my DM's? It's not happening!

Think about your purpose, if you don't know what yours is, think about the things you are good at and enjoy doing. Now look at every possible temptation that might come to destroy that. The temptations that you identified are the ones that you need to pray hard about. Ask God to show you someone that you can trust so they can help you break the strongholds with prayer. Ecclesiastes 4:9-10 (NLT) explains the reason we need accountability partners. The passage tells us:

"Two people are better off than one, for they can help each other succeed. If one person falls, the other can reach out and help. But someone who falls alone is in real trouble."

Along with prayer, you also have to adapt your behavior so you can avoid the temptation. One time, I was at the gas station and someone offered to pay for and pump my gas for me. I absolutely hate going to the gas station and more than going, I hate touching that filthy gas pump, so when someone offered to pump my gas I used to thank God. This particular time, I turned around and saw temptation wrapped in a Gray Nike Sweatsuit. I declined because I knew his game. He would pump my gas and try to "talk to" me. I enjoy being Mrs. Casillas, free gas was not worth losing my new name and everything that comes with it.

As I pulled the pump out of my car he sparked up a conversation about working out. He offered me his card, told me he was a personal trainer, and asked me to check out his Instagram. I took the card, said ok, and got in my car. As I drove down the street all I could do was laugh because I was thinking about the times when my friends and I would get approached by someone. If he sounded too perfect one of us would usually say, "Who sent him?". We weren't actually asking who sent him, that was our way of saying that he was trouble, too good to be true, or it was some kind of setup or shenanigan. This time I didn't even have to say who sent him. I knew exactly who sent him, that filthy devil. He knows exactly what I like and how I like it. He tried it, but I recognized the temptation because I had been there before. Because I was aware of my sin pattern, I knew how to handle the situation. I tossed that card right out the window!

Until I became aware of the strength that God gives during times of struggle, I felt defeated when I would fall to temptation. If you ask God to give you strength to resist temptation you have to believe that He will help you resist it.

Chapter 9 Journaling Questions

What do you think your purpose is? If you don't know, what are you good at?

In what ways does the enemy tempt you?

What are some ways you can resist temptation?

"Dear Heavenly Father, I am coming to you as your daughter and I am asking you to meet me here. You are King of Kings and Lord of Lords. There is no one or nothing greater than you. I thank you for the strength you have given me. The closer I get to you through spending time with you and reading your word, the stronger I will become. Thank you for giving me the power to resist the devil through your Holy Spirit that lives within me. Anytime temptation is before me I pray that I become more aware of your Spirit that will lead me away and help me resist temptation. I know that with Your help I will be able to make the right choices. I love you Daddy, thank you for everything, Amen."

10

He Loves You

You Are Seen

In such a big world, we can sometimes feel invisible or like we don't matter as much as someone else, but to God, you mean the world to Him! He put things in place specifically so that your individual story could occur. Every single move you have ever made is a part of the story that God created for you as an individual. There are people you have met that you will never forget. And although you might not think a particular interaction was important to someone you don't think about often, that person will never forget it. You may never see some individuals again, but I guarantee there is at least one person who remembers the words you said to them even if they weren't profound.

After graduating from college, I ran into someone I knew from middle school. I wasn't close to them, but their girlfriend's locker was next to mine, so I saw him daily. I don't remember having a conversation with him, but he expressed that the good morning I said to him every day helped him through a challenging time in his life. I didn't know that he was being bullied, leading him to be suicidal. He would lean on my locker every morning as he waited for his girlfriend. I initially began saying good morning so that he could get out of my way. I had no idea the impact of my good morning until eight years later when I learned that those two words made a more significant impact than I knew.

The enemy made this young man feel insignificant when he was younger because he was aware of the great things that God had intended to use him to accomplish. Satan figured if he could make him feel like he didn't matter, he could wipe him out early, and he wouldn't be able to fulfill God's purpose. But because God is always watching us, He makes sure things happen so that His plan is accomplished (Jeremiah 1:12). I think that God intentionally had him have a habit of leaning on my locker so that I would speak to him. I believe that God uses our actions to make sure His purpose is fulfilled. God had a great purpose lined up for that young man, and if he had never had the habit of leaning on my locker, I might have never said good morning to him. If I never said good morning to him, he may have felt even more insignificant and could've gone through with his plan to commit suicide. Today that young man plays a significant role in God's kingdom. He has worked with students to encourage them to go to college, he's a mentor to young black men, and he volunteers with many organizations across the city of Cleveland.

A story in the Bible talks about a shepherd with many sheep but notices that one of them is missing, and he leaves the herd of sheep to find that one lost sheep (Matthew 18:10-14). Hebrews 4:13 (ERV) says, "Nothing in all the world can be hidden from God. He can clearly see all things." These two passages are there to show you how important you are to God and how much He loves you. Sometimes you may feel small and unseen but remember God always has His eye on you. He is always watching and moving in the background on your behalf because you are filled with purpose.

You Are Needed

If you don't take anything else away from reading this book, I want you to know that your Heavenly Father loves you more than you will ever be able to comprehend. Every single move God makes is because He loves you and believes in you. God knows what you're capable of, even if you don't, and that is why He allows us to go through certain experiences that build our character. For example, in Exodus, God used Moses to free His people, but Moses was so insecure in his ability that he made excuses for why he couldn't do what God was asking him to do. Moses begged God to send someone else, but God didn't send someone in his place. Instead, he had Moses' brother help him (Exodus 4:13-17).

There are specific tasks that God is relying on you to complete because it's a part of the story He has written for you specifically. Although God sent Aaron with Moses to speak for Moses, God was still counting on Moses to complete the assigned tasks. God did not give Aaron the power to perform the miracles. He gave that power specifically to Moses. God has given you a specific purpose to complete so His grand purpose can be completed. You are a part of the bigger picture.

God is counting on you to do what He has called you to do and share parts of your story to help others get through their journeys and know God for themselves. God can use something as small as a good morning to ensure that someone reaches their destiny. If that young man from middle school had ended his life, there would've been plenty of individuals who may have never experienced the God in him. There would have been a lot of young men who chose street life over college, and I would've never learned the significance of something as small as a good morning.

Please be aware of the impact that you have on this world. You could be the reason why someone changes their life around, or you could be the reason why someone gives up on their dreams. You have no idea how much influence you have on the people around you. Don't ever think that you're too ordinary, too sinful, or too broken to be used by God for His purpose. God loves to use those people to get the job done. When God uses someone ordinary, broken, or sinful, God gets the glory because those people recognize it wasn't in their strength. They recognize that something happened, but God made it happen (Phillipians 2:13).

Let God Love You

As I said earlier, God has given us free will, and we have a choice to make. Will you let Him love you, or will you choose the path that leads to separation from His presence? God will always make a way for you to find Him. In Exodus 33, God was upset with the Israelites for their sinfulness. He told them to go on their way, but He would not go with them because He might've destroyed them because of how disappointed He was in them. Even in His anger, He made it possible for them to meet with Him by having Moses set up a meeting tent outside of the Israelite camp so that God could meet with them. God met with Moses in the tent, but the Israelites chose to wait for Moses to tell them what God said instead of going to the meeting tent themselves. Joshua, Moses' aide, was the only other person who chose to meet with God in the tent. I believe that Joshua became Moses' successor because He wanted to be with the Lord when no one else did. God blesses the ones who choose Him, especially those who choose Him when it seems like no one else is.

Psalm 84:11 says, "No good thing does he withhold from those who walk uprightly." When you love the Lord, you follow His commandments which means you are walking uprightly. With that being said, what's the worst that could happen from loving God? He blesses you, protects you, and guides you down a path filled with success? I don't know about you, but I don't see anything wrong with loving God.

I cannot close out this book without allowing you to dedicate or re-dedicate your life to the most incredible Father you will ever know. No matter if you've never had an intimate relationship with Him or if you have walked away, God is waiting for you with open arms, ready to love you. He wants you to open your heart to Him and receive everything He has in store for you. God wants to share His purpose with you and give you access to His kingdom, but first, you have to submit to His will and His way, which is not as hard as it sounds. All it takes is your surrender and giving Him the wheel.

The first thing you need to do is humble yourself. You have to recognize that God chose you long before you were born, and you are returning to Him (Ephesians 1:4). God always intended for you to be His. He was waiting on you to give up control and allow Him to lead. The most crucial part of giving your life over to God is believing in His son, Jesus Christ. Acts 16:30-31 explains that for you to be saved, you must believe in Jesus. If you don't acknowledge His son, you can't understand the sacrifice of love God made for you. If you don't appreciate his sacrifice, it's hard for you to understand and appreciate God's love for you. God allowed His only son to suffer so that Jesus can be used to forgive us of our sins and cleanse us with His blood (John 3:16-18). Without the forgiveness of sins and cleansing from the blood Jesus shed, we would never be able to be with God in Heaven.

Although Jesus died on the cross to forgive us of our sins, we have to confess our sins to Him and make an effort not to repeat the same mistakes (1 John 1:9). Salvation is a gift from God. It's not about how squeaky clean you are or about what you do. God gives you the grace to make mistakes, but you have to have enough faith and love for Him to know that your behavior must change, and the goal is to become more and more like Christ (Ephesians 2:8-9; Titus 3:5). The more love you have for God, the less likely you will disappoint Him by being disobedient, and the more Christ-like you become. The more Christ-like you become, the less likely you are to sin, and living for God becomes easier and easier because of the love you have for Him.

If you're ready to let God love you, I want you to open your heart and try to be as sincere as possible. Visualize yourself climbing into your Daddy God's lap and say the following to Him.

"Father God, I love you, and I thank you for choosing me to be your daughter. Thank you for seeing who I am and loving me more than I love myself. Sometimes I lose faith and stumble, but I thank you for being patient with me and never giving up on me. I thank you for sending your only son to Earth to die for my sins and to cleanse me with His blood so that I can live forever with You. I ask that You help me live a life that is pleasing to You. Please forgive me for my disobedience and I ask that you make me more aware of the things that break your heart so that I can change my ways and make you proud. Help me pay more attention to your Holy Spirit that helps me do what is right and stay away from what is wrong. I ask that each and every day Your Spirit shows me how to be more Christ-like and to embrace the talents and gifts that You have given me. Show me my purpose, and how to fulfill it so that I can bring You glory. I love You Daddy, and I thank You for everything. In Jesus' name I pray, Amen."

Now that you've chosen to let God love you, and to live for Him, expect your life to change. Expect God to pull on your heart so you can meet with Him daily. Look forward to His "Good morning" text. It comes in all forms. It might be an urge to read your Bible or a few scriptures in the morning, listen to a sermon, a Christian podcast, or listen to music, or the urge just to sit quietly with God. No matter how you do it just look forward to hearing from Him each morning because your "Good morning" text will be there waiting on you like clockwork.

Chapter 10 Journaling Questions

What have you learned about God from reading this book?

What have you learned about yourself?

What are you going to do to get closer to God?

"Dear Heavenly Father, you are the greatest father that a girl could ever ask for. You created an entire universe so that I would have somewhere to live. You have provided me with shelter, food, and water so that I can survive. You've blessed me with gifts, talents, intellect, and thoughts that are unique and make me special. You have orchestrated everything in my life to happen for my good and I thank you for your divine plan. Father, please forgive me for taking my relationship with you for granted. I ask that you seal everything that I have learned in my heart. I want my relationship with you to grow and become the most important relationship in my life. Show me the areas I need to surrender to you and who I may need to forgive. Lastly, I ask that you show me someone that needs to hear what I've learned so they can grow closer to you too. Daddy God I love you, and I thank you for everything, Amen."

All definitions were provided by Dictionary.com Unabridged Based on the Random House Unabridged Dictionary, © Random House, Inc. 2019 (unless noted otherwise)

The Five Love Languages, Gary Chapman Northfield Publishing, Chicago IL. (2010) p.77

LaMar Boschman, *The Rebirth of Music* (Bedford, Texas: Revival Press, 1980), p.11-12

Miemis, V. (2010, April 10). Essential Skills for 21st Century Survival: Part I: Pattern Recognition. Retrieved from Emergent by Design

As an educator, I discovered the importance of making something easy to comprehend. When people easily understand a thing, it's easier for them to apply what they learned.

As a social worker, I learned that many people have no idea how to use their moral compass to help guide them through life. There's an entire generation that desperately needs practical instruction that will save them from themselves.

As a counselor, I developed a better understanding of the emotional, mental, and spiritual needs of humans and the importance of communication and comprehension. Feeling understood is a vital part of a person's well-being.

Under the umbrella of Casillas Coaching I am able to fuse all three of my careers together and do exactly what I was created to do. At Casillas Coaching, we offer the tools and resources to help individuals, couples, and families become the best versions of themselves.

Coaching Services

Life Coaching
Relationship Coaching
Family Coaching

Curriculum & Study Materials

Self-Discovery Workbook Coloring Books

Inspirational Coaching Books
Good Morning Gorgeous: A Guide to Having an Intimate
Relationship with Your Heavenly Father

Please visit www.CASILLASCOACHING.com

for more information

or email at CasillasCoaching@gmail.com.